1 MONTH OF FREE READING

at
www.ForgottenBooks.com

By purchasing this book you are eligible for one month membership to ForgottenBooks.com, giving you unlimited access to our entire collection of over 1,000,000 titles via our web site and mobile apps.

To claim your free month visit:
www.forgottenbooks.com/free859431

ISBN 978-0-484-23183-1
PIBN 10859431

CARDUCCI

ALLE FONTI DEL CLITUMNO

GIOSUE · CARDUCCI
THE · SOURCES · OF · THE · CLITUMNUS.

TRANSLATION · AND · NOTES
BY · E. · J. · WATSON

J. W. ARROWSMITH LTD. BRISTOL
SIMPKIN. MARSHALL, HAMILTON, KENT
AND COMPANY LIMITED, LONDON
MDCCCCXII

CONTENTS.

PREFACE.

So far as I am aware this is the first appearance in an English dress of Carducci's Ode *Alle fonti del Clitumno*. Trezza calls it " incomparably beautiful for the unity of the rhythm and the thought that it expresses," and few people will be inclined to differ from this opinion. In the translation I have attempted to reproduce exactly the metre of the original. That such a magnificent evocation of antiquity should be practically unknown to the average English reader is my excuse for publishing it. The argument and the notes will, I hope, illustrate and elucidate some of the details of the poem.

My thanks are due to the firm of Zanichelli, in Bologna, for permission to use their copyright edition of Carducci. This will be of advantage to those who are able to enjoy the Ode in the Italian.

E. J. WATSON.

ARGUMENT.

THE scene opens on the mount hard by the sources of the Clitumnus. As of yore, the flocks come down, and the young Umbrian shepherd dips the sheep in the cold water. His mother sits at the cottage door and sings to her little baby. The thoughtful father, dressed in goat skins, like an ancient faun, guides the wagon drawn by beautiful white oxen, such oxen as Virgil loved (1–20).

Heavy hang the clouds on the Apennines that slope in a circle, and guard Umbria (20–24).

The poet, whose heart is stirred by love for the ancient country, and on whose brow the Italian gods flutter, invokes green Umbria and the god Clitumnus (24–28). He sings the praises of the weeping willow, of the ilex, and of the ivy, and shows the cypresses standing around the god like mighty sentries; and, amongst the shadows, Clitumnus sits and sings his songs (28–40).

But Umbria is attacked by other races,

and finally by Rome, who plants there her proud ensigns (40–48).

It is, however, Clitumnus, the common, indigenous god, who appeaseth the conquerors to the conquered, and through his caves it is that the cry rings calling the people together to fight against the mighty Hannibal (48–68). But although Hannibal defeats the Romans at Trasimenus, yet is he powerless against the little mountain town of Spoleto (68–76).

The poet now leaves the scenes of conflict and returns to the limpid pool of Clitumnus, and as he contemplates the water he sees the nymphs, and the naiads, and the dusky maidens of the mountain, dancing in the moonlight, and he hears the marriage song sung in honour of the nuptials of Janus and Camesena, the progenitors of the Italian people (76–104).

Then the scene changes. Clitumnus is dethroned, and only one temple remaineth to him (104–108). The pagan gods give place to the Galilean, who throws his cross into the arms of Rome (108–116). The nymphs flee to the trees and the mountains when they see a black-robed group wandering among the ruined temples, and hear them singing litanies. Over the deserted fields the strange crowd passes, and drags the people from the ploughs, and curses the spots that the divine sun blesses. The new sect raves in grottoes, and descends into the towns, and in delirium dances to the Crucified One (116–140).

The poet now evokes the siren of the Ilissus and that of the Tiber, and finishes with an apostrophe to Italy, the mother of bullocks for agriculture, and wild colts for battle, the ancient mother of corn and of vines, the Roman mother of eternal laws, and the mediæval mother of illustrious arts. To her he renews the chant of ancient praises, and the woods and the mountains and the rivers of Umbria applaud the song. With the whistling of steam, symbolic of renewed Italy, the Ode closes (140–156).

ALLE FONTI DEL CLITUMNO

TO THE SOURCES OF THE CLITUMNUS

ALLE FONTI DEL CLITUMNO.

Ancor dal monte, che di fóschi ondeggia
frassini al vento mormoranti e lunge
per l'aure odora fresco di silvestri
salvie e di timi,   4

scendon nel vespero umido, o Clitumno,
a te le greggi : a te l'umbro fanciullo
la riluttante pecora ne l'onda
immerge, mentre.   8

vèr' lui dal seno de la madre adusta,
che scalza siede al casolare e canta,
una poppante volgesi e dal viso
tondo sorride :   12

pensoso il padre, di caprine pelli
l'anche ravvolto come i fauni antichi,
regge il dipinto plaustro e la forza
de' bei giovenchi,   16

xiv

TO THE SOURCES OF THE CLITUMNUS.

Still from the mount, with darkly waving ashes
Murmuring unto the wind, and which, afar off
On the light breezes, smells fresh of the woodland
Sages and sweet thymes,

In the damp evening come down, O Clitumnus,
To thee the flocks : to thee the child of Umbria
The sheep reluctant into the cold water
Plunges and dips, whilst

From the dry bosom of the barefoot mother,
Who sits and sings there at the little homestead,
An infant turns towards him, and its round face
Ripples with sweet smiles.

Pensive the father, with the skins of young goats
Twisted about him like the fauns of old time,
Ruleth the painted wagon and the strength of
Beautiful oxen.

xv

de' bei giovenchi dal quadrato petto,
erti su 'l capo le lunate corna,
dolci ne gli occhi, nivei, che il mite
Virgilio amava.   20

Oscure intanto fumano le nubi
su l' Apennino : grande, austera, verde
de le montagne digradanti in cerchio
l' Umbria guarda.   24

Salve, Umbria verde, e tu del puro fonte
nume Clitumno ! Sento in cuor l' antica
patria e alleggiarmi su l' accesa fronte
gl' itali iddii.   28

Chi l' ombre indusse del piangente salcio
su' rivi sacri ? ti rapisca il vento
de l' Apennino, o molle pianta, amore
d' umili tempi !   32

Beautiful oxen with the breast square builded,
High on the head the curvèd horns erected,
Sweet in the eyes, and snowy, that the gentle
Virgil loved dearly.

Obscure and heavy meanwhile hang the dark clouds
On Apenninus : mighty, austere, verdant
From the fair mountains sloping down in circle
Umbria it guardeth.

Hail, Umbria verdant, and thou of the pure source
Divine Clitumnus. I feel in my heart's core
The ancient land, and fluttering on my hot brow
The gods Italian.

Who caused the shadows of the weeping willow
On sacred banks ? Let wind of Apenninus
Take thee by force, O gentle plant, O love of
Times that were humble !

Qui pugni a' verni e arcane istorie frema
co'l palpitante maggio ilice nera,
a cui d'allegra giovinezza il tronco
l'edera veste :   36

qui folti a torno l'emergente nume
stieno, giganti vigili, i cipressi ;
e tu fra l'ombre, tu fatali canta
carmi, o Clitumno.   40

O testimone di tre imperi, dinne
come il grave umbro ne' duelli atroce
cesse a l'astato velite e la forte
Etruria crebbe :   44

di' come sovra le congiunte ville
dal superato Cimino a gran passi
calò Gradivo poi, piantando i segni
fieri di Roma.   48

xviii

Here let the dusky ilex fight the winters
And secret stories shout with May vibrating,
Whose trunk with light and joyous youth the ivy
Tenderly dresses.

Here mighty crowds around the emerging god stand,
Tall giant sentries, cypresses in sable :
And thou amongst the shadows singest fatal
Songs, O Clitumnus.

O testimony of three Empires tells of
How the grave Umbrian in the fights atrocious
Yielded unto the lance armed soldier and then
Grew strong Etruria :

Tells of how on the cities that conjoin by
Conquered Ciminus swiftly then descended
Savage Gradivus, planting and uprearing
Proud Roman ensigns.

Ma tu placavi, indigete comune
italo nume, i vincitori a i vinti,
e quando tonò il punico furore
da 'l Trasimeno,   52

per gli antri tuoi sali grido, e la torta
lo ripercosse buccina da i monti :
—O tu che pasci i buoi presso Mevania
caliginosa,   56

e tu che i proni colli ari a la sponda
del Nar sinistra, e tu che i boschi abbatti
sovra Spoleto verdi o ne la marzia
Todi fai nozze,   60

lascia il bue grasso tra le canne, lascia
il torel fulvo a mezzo solco, lascia
ne l'inclinata quercia il cuneo, lascia
la sposa a l'ara ;   64

xx

But thou appeasest, common, humble, native,
Italian god, the conquerors to the conquered.
And when loud sounded the dread Punic thunder·
From Trasimenus,

Through thy dark caves the cry rose, and the twisted
Trumpet returned it ringing from the mountains :
—O thou who pasturest the white patient oxen
Near dim Mevania,

And thou who ploughest the prone hills to the light wav
Of the left Nar, and thou who fellest the forests
O'er green Spoleto or who in the march makest
Marriage with Todi,

Leave thou the fat ox 'mongst the reeds, and also
Leave thou the tawny bull mid-furrow, leave thou
In falling oak the wedge, and also leave the
Bride at the altar ;

e corri, corri, corri! con la scure
corri e co' dardi, con la clava e l'asta!
corri! minaccia gl'itali penati
Annibal diro.—   68

Deh come rise d'alma luce il sole
per questa chiostra di bei monti, quando
urlanti vide e ruinanti in fuga
l'alta Spoleto   72

i Mauri immani e i numidi cavalli
con mischia oscena, e, sovra loro, nembi
di ferro, flutti d'olio ardente, e i canti
de la vittoria!   76

Tutto ora tace. Nel sereno gorgo
la tenue miro saliente vena:
trema, e d'un lieve pullular lo specchio
segna de l'acque.   80

xxii

And run thou, run thou, run thou ! with the fierce ax
Run thou with darts, with clubs and with the sharp lance
Run thou ! for threats the Italian penates
Hannibal dreaded.—

Ah ! me, how laughed with fostering light the sun throug
This cloister of fair mountains, when it looked on
Lofty Spoleto shouting and o'erthrowing
In flight the mighty

Mauri, and also the Numidian horses
In ghastly conflict, and above them, showers
Of iron, waves of burning oil, and glad songs
Of glorious victory !

All now is silent. In the placid whirlpool
The vein so slender splendid and surprising
Trembles, and with a movement light the mirror
Tells of the water.

Ride sepolta a l'imo una foresta
breve, e rameggia immobile : il diaspro
par che si mischi in flessuosi amori
con l'ametista.   84

E di zaffiro i fior paiono, ed hanno
de l'adamante rigido i riflessi,
e splendon freddi e chiamano a i silenzi
del verde fondo.   88

A piè de i monti e de le querce a l'ombra
Co' fiumi, o Italia, è de' tuoi carmi il fonte.
Visser le ninfe, vissero : e un divino
talamo è questo.   92

Emergean lunghe ne' fluenti veli
naiadi azzurre, e per la cheta sera
chiamavan alto le sorelle brune
da le montagne,   96

Deep at the bottom laughs a little forest,
And spreads its branches motionless : the jasper
Seems for to join itself in flexuous loves with
Amethyst splendid.

The flowers appear as if of sapphire, and have
Reflexions from the rigid adamant, and
Shine cold and clear, and call unto the silence
Of the green deepness.

At feet of mounts, and oaks, in shade by rivers,
O Italy, the source of thy songs springeth.
Here lived the nymphs, they lived : and what a holy
Nuptial bed this is.

Emerged at length in flowing veils blue naiads,
And through the soft and quiet evening loudly
Called they, inviting the sweet dusky sisters
Down from the mountains,

e danze sotto l' imminente luna
guidavan, liete ricantando in coro
di Giano eterno e quanto amor lo vinse
di Camesena.   100

Egli dal cielo, autoctona virago
ella : fu letto l' Apennin fumante :
velaro i nembi il grande amplesso, e nacque
l' itala gente.   104

Tutto ora tace, o vedovo Clitumno,
tutto : de' vaghi tuoi delúbri un solo
t' avanza, e dentro pretestato nume
tu non vi siedi.   108

Non piú perfusi del tuo fiume sacro
menano i tori, vittime orgogliose,
trofei romani a i templi aviti : Roma
piú non trionfa.   112

xxvi   ·

And in the moonlight guided they the dances,
Joyously hymning in delightful chorus
Janus eternal and how Camesena
By love subdued him.

From heaven he, autochtonous virago
She : Appeninus was their bed ; and storm clouds
Concealed the loved clasp, and the Italian people
Thus were conceivèd.

All now is silent, O Clitumnus widowed,
All. Of thy lovely temples one alone now
To thee remaineth, and a vested god there
Thou no more sittest.

No more besprinkled with thy sacred river
Lead they the white bulls, proud and patient victims,
Rich Roman trophies to the temples ancient :
Rome no more triumphs.

Piú non trionfa, poi che un galileo
di rosse chiome il Campidoglio ascese,
gittolle in braccio una sua croce, e disse
— Portala, e servi.—   116

Fuggir le ninfe a piangere ne' fiumi
occulte e dentro i cortici materni,
od ululándo dileguaron come
nùvole a i monti,   120

quando una strana compagnia, tra i bianchi
templi spogliati e i colonnati infranti,
procedé lenta, in neri sacchi avvolta,
litaniando,   124

e sovra i campi del lavoro umano
sonanti e i clivi memori d' impero
fece deserto, et il deserto disse
regno di Dio.   128

xxviii

Triumphs no more, since that a Galilean
With red hair mounted to the Capitolium,
Threw in her arms one of his crosses, saying
— Bear it, and serve thou.—

Swift fled the nymphs to sorrow in the secret
Rivers and deep within the barks maternal,
Or with fear screaming vanished they in crowds like
Clouds to the mountains,

When a strange group, between the old white temples
Plundered and ruined, and the broken columns,
Proceeded slowly, in black robes enveloped,
Litanies singing,

And o'er the fields of human labour telling,
And the slopes mindful of stupendous empire
Made bare and desert, and the desert cried out,
This is God's kingdom.

xxix

Strappâr le turbe a i santi aratri, a i vecchi
padri aspettanti, a le fiorenti mogli ;
ovunque il divo sol benedicea,
maledicenti.   132

Maledicenti a l' opre de la vita
e de l' amore, ei deliraro atroci
congiugnimenti di dolor con Dio
su rupi e in grotte :   136

discesero ebri di dissolvimento
a le cittadi, e in ridde paurose
al crocefisso supplicarono, empi,
d' esser abietti.   140

Salve, o serena de l' Ilisso in riva,
o intera e dritta a i lidi almi del Tebro
anima umana ! i fóschi dí passaro,
risorgi e regna.   144

xxx

They dragged the crowds away from holy ploughs, from
Old fathers waiting, and from fruitful spouses :
And every place the sun divine was blessing,
Banning and cursing.

Cursing the works of life and also cursing
The works of love : they raved in mad delirium
Atrocious things conjoining grief with God on
Rocks and in grottos :   . ,

Drunk they descended, drunk to dissolution
Into the cities, and in round dance fearful
Cried supplications to the crucified one,
Impious, being abjects.

Hail, siren on the banks of the Ilissus,
Or honest, upright, human soul, on fostering
Shores of the Tiber ! the dark days evanish,
Arise and reign thou.

E tu, pia madre di giovenchi invitti
a franger glebe e rintegrar maggesi
e d' annitrenti in guerra aspri polledri
Italia madre,   148

madre di biade e viti e leggi eterne
ed inclite arti a raddolcir la vita,
salve! a te i canti de l' antica lode
io rinnovello.   152

Plaudono i monti al carme e i boschi e l'acque
de l'Umbria verde : in faccia a noi fumando
ed anelando nuove industrie in corsa
fischia il vapore.   156

And thou, O pious mother of unvanquished
Bullocks to break glebe and restore lands fallow,
And of fierce colts for neighing in the battle :
Italy mother,

Mother of corn and vines and of eternal
Laws and illustrious arts the life to sweeten,
Hail, hail, all hail ! the songs of ancient praises
Renew I to thee.

The mountains, woods, and waters of green Umbria
Applaud the song : and here before us fuming
And longing for new industries aracing
Whistles the white steam.

NOTES

NOTES.

To the Sources of the Clitumnus.—The Clitumnus is
a small river in Umbria, springing from a beautiful
rock in a grove of cypress trees, where was a sanctuary
of the god Clitumnus, and falling into the Tinia, a
tributary of the Tiber.—Smith's *Classical Dict.*, 120.

Pliny knew the Sources well, and wrote the following
delightful letter to his friend Romanus on the subject
(*Epist.* iii, 8) :—

" Have you ever seen the source of the Clitumnus ?
I suppose not, as I never heard you mention it. Let
me advise you to go there at once. I have just seen it,
and am sorry I put off my visit so long. At the foot
of a little hill, covered with old and shady cypress trees,
gushes out a spring, which bursts out into a number of
streamlets, all of different sizes. Having struggled, so
to speak, out of its confinement, it opens out into a
broad basin, so clear and transparent that you may
count the pebbles and little pieces of money which
are thrown into it. From this point the force and
weight of the water, rather than the slope of the ground,
hurries it onward. What was a mere fountain becomes
a noble river, wide enough to allow vessels to pass each
other, as they sail with or against the stream. The

current is so strong, though the ground is level, that large barges, as they go down the river, do not require the assistance of oars; while to go up it is as much as can possibly be done with oars and long poles. When you sail up and down for amusement, the ease of going down the stream and the labour of returning make a pleasant variety. The banks are clothed with an abundance of ash and poplar, which are so distinctly reflected in the clear water that they seem to be growing at the bottom of the river, and can be easily counted. The water is as cold as snow, and its colour the same. Near it stands an ancient and venerable temple, in which is a statue of the river-god Clitumnus, clothed in the usual robe of state. The oracles here delivered attest the presence of the deity. In the immediate neighbourhood are several little chapels, dedicated to particular gods, each of whom has his distinctive name and special worship, and is the tutelary deity of a fountain. For, besides the principal spring, which is, as it were, the parent of all the rest, there are several smaller springs, which have a distinct source, but which unite their waters with the Clitumnus, over which a bridge is thrown, separating the sacred part of the river from that which is open to general use. Above the bridge you may only go in a boat; below it, you may swim. The people of the town of Hispallum, to whom Augustus gave this place, furnish baths and lodgings at the public expense. There are several little houses on the banks, in the specially picturesque situations, and they are quite close to the water. In short, everything in the neighbourhood will give you pleasure. You may also amuse yourself with numberless inscriptions on the pillars and walls, celebrating the praises of the stream and of its tutelary divinity. Many of these you will admire, and some will make you laugh. But no ; you are too cultivated a person to laugh on such an occasion. Farewell."

line 22. *Apenninus.*—Mons Apenninus ; the Apennines.

line 25. *Hail, Umbria verdant.*—Umbria, called by the Greeks *Ombrica*, a district of Italy, bounded on the north by Gallia Cisalpina, from which it was separated by the River Rubicon ; on the east by the Adriatic Sea ; on the south by the Rivers Aesis and Nar ; and on the west by the Tiber. The chief towns were Ariminum, Fanum Fortunæ, Mevania, Tuder, Narnia, and Spoletium.

> " Bear me, some god, to Baiæ's gentle seats,
> Or cover me in Umbria's green retreats ;
> Where western gales eternally reside,

And all the seasons lavish all their pride :
Blossoms and fruits and flowers together rise,
And the whole year in gay confusion lies."

Addison, Letter from Italy.

line 42. *The grave Umbrian.*—The Umbri were one of the most ancient and powerful peoples in central Italy. They were afterwards deprived of their possessions west of the Tiber by the Etruscans, and their territories were still further diminished by the Senones. The Umbri were subdued by the Romans B.C. 307. After the conquest of the Senones by the Romans in 283 they again obtained possession of the country on the coast of the Adriatic.—Smith's *Classical Dict.,* 445.

line 44. *Strong Etruria.*—Etruria proper was bounded on the north and north-west by the Apennines and the River Macra, which divided it from Liguria, on the west by the Tyrrhene Sea or Mare Inferum, and on the east and south by the River Tiber, which separated it from Umbria and Latium. The Etruscans were a very powerful nation when Rome was still in its infancy.—Smith's *Classical Dict.,* 161.

line 46. *Conquered Ciminus.*—The Etruscans declared war against Rome in 311 B.C. Fabius, the Consul, determined to enter Upper Etruria. For this purpose it was necessary to traverse the Ciminian forest. So dreaded was this spot that the Senate sent legates to Fabius charging him not to enter the wood (Livy, ix, 36). The Consul, however, sent his brother Marcus to examine the country beyond, and this having been done, Fabius entered the dreaded place and ravaged the country far and wide. All Rome was terror-struck at the act.—Livy, ix, 38.

" Cimini cum monte lacum."

Virgil, *Æneid* vii, 695.

line 47. *Gradivus.*—A surname of Mars.

line 52. *Trasimenus.*—Lake Trasimenus is associated with Hannibal's famous victory over Flaminius, 217 B.C. In this battle fifteen thousand Romans fell. Livy tells us that during the conflict an earthquake occurred, but so intent were the combatants that it was not felt by one of them.—Livy, xxii, 4–7.

" Namque ego sum celsis quem cinctum montibus ambit
Tmolo missa manus, stagnis Thrasymenus opacis."

Silius Italicus, iv, 737.

　　　　　　　　　　　　" I roam
By Thrasimene's lake, in the defiles
Fatal to Roman rashness, more at home ;
For there the *Carthaginian's* warlike wiles
Come back before me, as his skill beguiles
The host between the mountains and the shore,
Where *Courage* falls in her despairing files,
And torrents, swoll'n to rivers with their gore,
Reek through the sultry plain, with legions scatter'd o'er,

Like to a forest fell'd by mountain winds ;
And such the storm of battle on this day,
And such the frenzy, whose convulsion blinds
To all save carnage, that, beneath the fray,
An earthquake reel'd unheededly away !
None felt stern Nature rocking at his feet,
And yawning forth a grave for those who lay
Upon their bucklers for a winding sheet ;
Such is the absorbing hate when warring nations meet !
　　　　　　　　Childe Harold, c, iv, *vv,* lxii, lxiii.

line 56. *Mevania.*—Mevania, now Bevagna, a town
about six miles from Foligno. Propertius was probably
born there.

　　　" Mevania, latis projecta in campis."
　　　　　　　　　　　Silius Italicus, vi, 644.

line 58. *The left Nar.*—The River Nar traverses a

vale of most delightful appearance. Its wave washes the base of the very high and steep hill on which stands Narni. Virgil (*Æneid*, vii, 518) calls it *Sulfurea Nar albus aqua.*

line 59. *Spoleto.*—In 217 B.C. Hannibal attacked Spoleto after he had conquered the Romans at the Battle of Trasimenus, but the inhabitants repulsed the great Carthaginian general.

line 60. *Todi.*—Todi occupies the site of the ancient *Tuder,* whose lofty position is mentioned by Silius Italieus, iv, 222—

" Gradivicolam celso de colle Tudertem "
and vi, 645—
". . . excelso summum qua vertice montis
  Devexum lateri pendet Tuder."

line 67. *The Italian Penates.*—The Penates were the household gods of the Romans, both those of a private family and of the State. They were kept in the *penetralia.* The Lares were included among the Penates. Most ancient writers believed that the Penates of the State were brought by Æneas from Troy into Italy, and were preserved first at Lavinium, afterwards at Alba Longa, and finally at Rome. The private Penates had their place at the hearth of every house, and the table also was sacred to them. On the hearth a perpetual fire was kept up in their honour, and the table always contained the salt-cellar and the firstlings of fruit for these divinities.—Smith's *Classical Dict.*, 309.

There were four *Penates* of Etrusca—*Ceres*, *Pales*, *Fortuna*, and the *Genius Jovalis* (*Arnob. adv. Nat.*, iii, 40, *Serv. ad Æn.*, ii, 325) ; and the two *Penates* of Latium—the Dioscuri—*Castur* and *Pultuke*—were much worshipped in Etruria, as we learn from monuments.—Dennis, *Cities and Cemeteries of Etruria*, i, 34.

line 73. *The Mauri.*—The Mauri were the inhabitants of Mauretania, a country in the north of Africa. Numidia bounded it on the east.

line 77. *All now is silent*—

But thou, Clitumnus, in thy sweetest wave
Of the most living crystal that was e'er
The haunt of river nymph, to gaze and lave
Her limbs where nothing hid them, thou dost rear
Thy grassy banks whereon the milk-white steer
Grazes ; the purest god of gentle waters !

And most serene of aspect, and most clear ;
Surely that stream was unprofaned by slaughters—
A mirror and a bath for Beauty's youngest daughters !

And on thy happy shore a Temple still,
Of small and delicate proportion, keeps,
Upon a mild declivity of hill
Its memory of thee : beneath it sweeps
Thy current's calmness ; oft from out it leaps
The finny darter with the glittering scales,
Who dwells and revels in thy glassy deeps ;
While, chance, some scatter'd water-lily sails
Down where the shallower wave still tells its bubbling
     tales.

Pass not unblest the Genius of the place !
If through the air a zephyr more serene
Win to the brow, 'tis his ; and if ye trace
Along his margin a more eloquent green,
If on the heart the freshness of the scene
Sprinkle its coolness, and from the dry dust
Of weary life a moment lave it clean
With Nature's baptism—'tis to him ye must
Pay orisons for this suspension of disgust.

            Childe Harold, c, iv, *vv*, lxvi–lxviii.

line 99. *Janus eternal.*—Janus was a Latin divinity,
who was worshipped as the sun. The name *Janus* is

only another form of *Dianus*. He is commonly represented with two heads, and sometimes with four heads. Dennis refers to him as an Etruscan god, but says he may have been of foreign introduction (*Cities and Cemeteries of Etruria*, i, 33). A four-faced Janus was worshipped at Falerii (*Serv. ad Æn.*, vii).

line 106. *Of thy lovely temples one alone now . . . remaineth.*—This temple consists of the cella and a Corinthian portico, supported by four pillars and two pilasters; the pilasters are fluted; two of the pillars are indented with two spiral lines winding round and two ornamented with a light sculpture representing the scales of fish. The inscription on the frieze is singular: "*Deus angelorum, qui fecit resurrectionem.*" Underneath is a vault or crypt: the entrance is on the side, as the portico hangs over the river; the walls are solid, the proportions beautiful, and the whole worthy of the Romans, to whom it is ascribed.—Eustace, *Classical Tour*, i, 225.

line 109. *No more besprinkled with thy sacred river.*—
Hine albi, Clitumne greges et maxima taurus
Victima, sæpe tuo perfusi flumine sacro,
Romanos ad templa deum duxere triumphos.

Milk-white herds, O fair Clitumnus,
    bathe them in thy sacred tide—
Mighty bulls to crown the altars, or
    to draw the conqueror's car
Up the Sacred Way in triumph, when
    he rideth from the war.

               Virgil, *Georg.* ii, 146, Collins' Trans.

line 114. *The Capitolium.*—The Capitolium was the temple of Jupiter Optimus Maximus at Rome, situated on the south summit of the Mons Capitolinus.

line 141. *Hail siren . . . of the Ilissus.*—The Ilissus is a small river in Attica, rising on the north slope of Mount Hymettus, and flowing through the east side of Athens.

CPSIA information can be obtained
at www.ICGtesting.com
Printed in the USA
BVHW04*1123160818

524721BV00023B/2346/P

9 780484 231831